SHAKESPEARE
ON LOVE

Verona anno 303.

Shake

on

COMPILED BY

peare

Love

BENJAMIN
DARLING

PRENTICE HALL PRESS

PRINTED IN THE UNITED STATES OF AMERICA.

10   9   8   7   6   5   4   3   2   1

ISBN   0-7352-0174-9

PRENTICE HALL PRESS

http://www phdirect com

Rosalind and Celia

A Midsummer Night's Dream

TITANIA

I PRAY THEE, GENTLE MORTAL, SING AGAIN:
MINE EAR IS MUCH ENAMOUR'D OF THY NOTE;
SO IS MINE EYE ENTHRALLED TO THY SHAPE;
AND THY FAIR VIRTUE'S FORCE PERFORCE DOTH MOVE ME
ON THE FIRST VIEW TO SAY, TO SWEAR, I LOVE THEE.

BOTTOM

METHINKS, MISTRESS, YOU SHOULD HAVE LITTLE REASON
FOR THAT: AND YET, TO SAY THE TRUTH, REASON AND
LOVE KEEP LITTLE COMPANY TOGETHER NOW-A-DAYS; THE
MORE THE PITY THAT SOME HONEST NEIGHBOURS WILL NOT
MAKE THEM FRIENDS. NAY, I CAN GLEEK UPON OCCASION.

TITANIA

THOU ART AS WISE AS THOU ART BEAUTIFUL.

Shakespeare on Love—could there be a more felicitous pairing of subject with author? From his most sparkling comedies to his darkest tragedies and in his 154 sonnets, the Bard contemplated love in all its various forms. From the witty banter of Beatrice and Benedick, to the youthful passion of Romeo and Juliet, Shakespeare's treatment of this universal subject is both wide in its sweep and has remained remarkably relevant for nearly 400 years. In *Shakespeare on Love* I have selected from amongst Shakespeare's best and best known quotes on love and lovers and paired them with beautiful and apt illustrations from the many artists and illustrators who have put pen and brush to this great subject. The Bard himself said "By Heaven, I do love, and it hath taught me to rime"—it is my hope that readers will find *Shakespeare on Love* to be an entertaining volume that showcases Britain's greatest author on humankind's most absorbing topic.

—*Benjamin Darling*

Sonnet 116

LET ME NOT TO THE MARRIAGE OF TRUE MINDS
ADMIT IMPEDIMENTS; LOVE IS NOT LOVE
WHICH ALTERS WHEN IT ALTERATION FINDS,
OR BENDS WITH THE REMOVER TO REMOVE.
OH, NO, IT IS AN EVER-FIXED MARK,
THAT LOOKS ON TEMPESTS AND IS NEVER SHAKEN;
IT IS THE STAR TO EVERY WAND'RING BARK,
WHOSE WORTH'S UNKNOWN, ALTHOUGH HIS HEIGHT BE TAKEN.
LOVE'S NOT TIME'S FOOL, THOUGH ROSY LIPS AND CHEEKS
WITHIN HIS BENDING SICKLE'S COMPASS COME;
LOVE ALTERS NOT WITH HIS BRIEF HOURS AND WEEKS,
BUT BEARS IT OUT EVEN TO THE EDGE OF DOOM.
IF THIS BE ERROR, AND UPON ME PROVED,
I NEVER WRIT, NOR NO MAN EVER LOVED.

A Midsummer Night's Dream

LOVE LOOKS NOT WITH THE EYES, BUT WITH THE MIND;
AND THEREFORE IS WING'D CUPID PAINTED BLIND.

NO SOONER MET BUT THEY LOOKED,
NO SOONER LOOKED BUT THEY LOVED,
NO SOONER LOVED BUT THEY SIGHED,
NO SOONER SIGHED BUT THEY ASKED ONE ANOTHER THE REASON,
NO SOONER KNEW THE REASON BUT THEY SOUGHT THE REMEDY.

BREAK AN HOUR'S PROMISE IN LOVE!
HE THAT WILL DIVIDE A MINUTE INTO A THOUSAND PARTS
AND BREAK BUT A PART OF THE THOUSANDTH PART OF A MINUTE
IN THE AFFAIRS OF LOVE, IT MAY BE SAID OF HIM
THAT CUPID HATH CLAPPED HIM O' THE SHOULDER,
BUT I'LL WARRANT HIM HEART-WHOLE.

COME, GENTLE NIGHT, COME, LOVING, BLACK-BROW'D NIGHT,
GIVE ME MY ROMEO; AND, WHEN HE SHALL DIE,
TAKE HIM AND CUT HIM OUT IN LITTLE STARS,
AND HE WILL MAKE THE FACE OF HEAVEN SO FINE
THAT ALL THE WORLD WILL BE IN LOVE WITH NIGHT
AND PAY NO WORSHIP TO THE GARISH SUN.
O, I HAVE BOUGHT THE MANSION OF A LOVE,
BUT NOT POSSESS'D IT, AND, THOUGH I AM SOLD,
NOT YET ENJOY'D: SO TEDIOUS IS THIS DAY
AS IS THE NIGHT BEFORE SOME FESTIVAL
TO AN IMPATIENT CHILD THAT HATH NEW ROBES
AND MAY NOT WEAR THEM.

Hamlet

DOUBT THOU THE STARS ARE FIRE;
DOUBT THAT THE SUN DOTH MOVE;
DOUBT TRUTH TO BE A LIAR;
BUT NEVER DOUBT I LOVE.

Sonnet 18

SHALL I COMPARE THEE TO A SUMMER'S DAY?
THOU ART MORE LOVELY AND MORE TEMPERATE:
ROUGH WINDS DO SHAKE THE DARLING BUDS OF MAY,
AND SUMMER'S LEASE HATH ALL TOO SHORT A DATE.

The Tempest

FAIR ENCOUNTER OF TWO MOST RARE AFFECTIONS!
HEAVENS RAIN GRACE ON THAT WHICH BREEDS BETWEEN 'EM!

The Two Gentlemen of Verona

WHO IS SILVIA? WHAT IS SHE,
THAT ALL OUR SWAINS COMMEND HER?
HOLY, FAIR AND WISE IS SHE;
THE HEAVEN SUCH GRACE DID LEND HER,
THAT SHE MIGHT ADMIRED BE.

IS SHE KIND AS SHE IS FAIR?
FOR BEAUTY LIVES WITH KINDNESS.
LOVE DOTH TO HER EYES REPAIR,
TO HELP HIM OF HIS BLINDNESS,
AND, BEING HELP'D, INHABITS THERE.

THEN TO SILVIA LET US SING,
THAT SILVIA IS EXCELLING;
SHE EXCELS EACH MORTAL THING
UPON THE DULL EARTH DWELLING:
TO HER LET US GARLANDS BRING.

The Merry Wives of Windsor

WHAT MADE ME LOVE THEE? LET THAT PERSUADE THEE
THERE'S SOMETHING EXTRAORDINARY IN THEE.
COME, I CANNOT COG AND SAY THOU ART THIS AND THAT,
LIKE A MANY OF THESE LISPING HAWTHORN-BUDS,
THAT COME LIKE WOMEN IN MEN'S APPAREL,
AND SMELL LIKE BUCKLERSBURY IN SIMPLE TIME;
I CANNOT: BUT I LOVE THEE;
NONE BUT THEE; AND THOU DESERVEST IT.

BUT, SOFT! WHAT LIGHT THROUGH YONDER WINDOW BREAKS?
IT IS THE EAST, AND JULIET IS THE SUN.
ARISE, FAIR SUN, AND KILL THE ENVIOUS MOON,
WHO IS ALREADY SICK AND PALE WITH GRIEF,
THAT THOU HER MAID ART FAR MORE FAIR THAN SHE:
BE NOT HER MAID, SINCE SHE IS ENVIOUS;
HER VESTAL LIVERY IS BUT SICK AND GREEN
AND NONE BUT FOOLS DO WEAR IT; CAST IT OFF.
IT IS MY LADY, O, IT IS MY LOVE!

As You Like It

WHO EVER LOVED THAT LOVED NOT AT FIRST SIGHT?

27

GOOD NIGHT, GOOD NIGHT! PARTING IS SUCH SWEET SORROW,
THAT I SHALL SAY GOOD NIGHT TILL IT BE MORROW.

SHAKESPEARE ❨ ON LOVE

Troilus and Cressida

TO BE WISE AND LOVE EXCEEDS MAN'S MIGHT.

A Midsummer Night's Dream

AY ME! FOR AUGHT THAT I COULD EVER READ,
COULD EVER HEAR BY TALE OR HISTORY,
THE COURSE OF TRUE LOVE NEVER DID RUN SMOOTH.

SEE, HOW SHE LEANS HER CHEEK UPON HER HAND!
O, THAT I WERE A GLOVE UPON THAT HAND,
THAT I MIGHT TOUCH THAT CHEEK!

As You Like It

COME, WOO ME, WOO ME, FOR NOW I AM IN A HOLIDAY
HUMOUR AND LIKE ENOUGH TO CONSENT.

Twelfth Night

IF EVER THOU SHALT LOVE,
IN THE SWEET PANGS OF IT REMEMBER ME;
FOR SUCH AS I AM ALL TRUE LOVERS ARE,
UNSTAID AND SKITTISH IN ALL MOTIONS ELSE,
SAVE IN THE CONSTANT IMAGE OF THE CREATURE
THAT IS BELOVED.

Othello

I HUMBLY DO BESEECH YOU OF YOUR PARDON
FOR TOO MUCH LOVING YOU.

IT WAS A LOVER AND HIS LASS,
WITH A HEY, AND A HO, AND A HEY NONINO,
THAT O'ER THE GREEN CORN-FIELD DID PASS
IN THE SPRING TIME, THE ONLY PRETTY RING TIME,
WHEN BIRDS DO SING, HEY DING A DING, DING:
SWEET LOVERS LOVE THE SPRING.

BETWEEN THE ACRES OF THE RYE,
WITH A HEY, AND A HO, AND A HEY NONINO
THESE PRETTY COUNTRY FOLKS WOULD LIE,
IN THE SPRING TIME, THE ONLY PRETTY RING TIME,
WHEN BIRDS DO SING, HEY DING A DING, DING:
SWEET LOVERS LOVE THE SPRING.

THIS CAROL THEY BEGAN THAT HOUR,
WITH A HEY, AND A HO, AND A HEY NONINO,
HOW THAT A LIFE WAS BUT A FLOWER
IN THE SPRING TIME, THE ONLY PRETTY RING TIME,
WHEN BIRDS DO SING, HEY DING A DING, DING:
SWEET LOVERS LOVE THE SPRING.

AND THEREFORE TAKE THE PRESENT TIME,
WITH A HEY, AND A HO, AND A HEY NONINO;
FOR LOVE IS CROWNED WITH THE PRIME
IN THE SPRING TIME, THE ONLY PRETTY RING TIME,
WHEN BIRDS DO SING, HEY DING A DING, DING:
SWEET LOVERS LOVE THE SPRING.

The Taming of the Shrew

THIS DONE, HE TOOK THE BRIDE ABOUT THE NECK
AND KISS'D HER LIPS WITH SUCH A CLAMOROUS SMACK
THAT AT THE PARTING ALL THE CHURCH DID ECHO.

Much Ado about Nothing

BENEDICK

I PRAY THEE NOW, TELL ME FOR WHICH OF MY BAD PARTS
DIDST THOU FIRST FALL IN LOVE WITH ME?

BEATRICE

FOR WHICH OF MY GOOD PARTS
DID YOU FIRST SUFFER LOVE FOR ME?

Romeo and Juliet

DID MY HEART LOVE TILL NOW? FORSWEAR IT, SIGHT!
FOR I NE'ER SAW TRUE BEAUTY TILL THIS NIGHT.

As You Like It

PHEBE

GOOD SHEPHERD, TELL THIS YOUTH WHAT 'TIS TO LOVE.

SILVIUS

IT IS TO BE ALL MADE OF SIGHS AND TEARS; . . .
IT IS TO BE ALL MADE OF FAITH AND SERVICE; . . .
IT IS TO BE ALL MADE OF FANTASY,
ALL MADE OF PASSION AND ALL MADE OF WISHES,
ALL ADORATION, DUTY, AND OBSERVANCE,
ALL HUMBLENESS, ALL PATIENCE AND IMPATIENCE,
ALL PURITY, ALL TRIAL, ALL OBSERVANCE.

IF MUSIC BE THE FOOD OF LOVE, PLAY ON;
GIVE ME EXCESS OF IT, THAT, SURFEITING,
THE APPETITE MAY SICKEN, AND SO DIE.
THAT STRAIN AGAIN! IT HAD A DYING FALL:
O, IT CAME O'ER MY EAR LIKE THE SWEET SOUND,
THAT BREATHES UPON A BANK OF VIOLETS,
STEALING AND GIVING ODOUR!

A Midsummer Night's Dream

AND I DO LOVE THEE: THEREFORE, GO WITH ME;
I'LL GIVE THEE FAIRIES TO ATTEND ON THEE,
AND THEY SHALL FETCH THEE JEWELS FROM THE DEEP,
AND SING WHILE THOU ON PRESSED FLOWERS DOST SLEEP.

Love's Labours Lost

BUT LOVE, FIRST LEARNED IN A LADY'S EYES,
LIVES NOT ALONE IMMURED IN THE BRAIN;
BUT, WITH THE MOTION OF ALL ELEMENTS,
COURSES AS SWIFT AS THOUGHT IN EVERY POWER,
AND GIVES TO EVERY POWER A DOUBLE POWER,
ABOVE THEIR FUNCTIONS AND THEIR OFFICES.
IT ADDS A PRECIOUS SEEING TO THE EYE;
A LOVER'S EYES WILL GAZE AN EAGLE BLIND;
A LOVER'S EAR WILL HEAR THE LOWEST SOUND,
WHEN THE SUSPICIOUS HEAD OF THEFT IS STOPP'D:
LOVE'S FEELING IS MORE SOFT AND SENSIBLE
THAN ARE THE TENDER HORNS OF COCKL'D SNAILS;
LOVE'S TONGUE PROVES DAINTY BACCHUS GROSS IN TASTE:
FOR VALOUR, IS NOT LOVE A HERCULES,
STILL CLIMBING TREES IN THE HESPERIDES?
SUBTLE AS SPHINX; AS SWEET AND MUSICAL
AS BRIGHT APOLLO'S LUTE, STRUNG WITH HIS HAIR:
AND WHEN LOVE SPEAKS, THE VOICE OF ALL THE GODS
MAKES HEAVEN DROWSY WITH THE HARMONY.
NEVER DURST POET TOUCH A PEN TO WRITE
UNTIL HIS INK WERE TEMPER'D WITH LOVE'S SIGHS;
O, THEN HIS LINES WOULD RAVISH SAVAGE EARS
AND PLANT IN TYRANTS MILD HUMILITY.
FROM WOMEN'S EYES THIS DOCTRINE I DERIVE:
THEY SPARKLE STILL THE RIGHT PROMETHEAN FIRE;
THEY ARE THE BOOKS, THE ARTS, THE ACADEMES,
THAT SHOW, CONTAIN AND NOURISH ALL THE WORLD:
ELSE NONE AT ALL IN OUGHT PROVES EXCELLENT.

Troilus and Cressida

THE KISS YOU TAKE IS BETTER THAN YOU GIVE.

Troilus and Cressida

MY HEART BEATS THICKER THAN A FEVEROUS PULSE;
AND ALL MY POWERS DO THEIR BESTOWING LOSE,
LIKE VASSALAGE AT UNAWARES ENCOUNTERING
THE EYE OF MAJESTY.

As You Like It

THE SIGHT OF LOVERS FEEDETH THOSE IN LOVE.

The Two Gentlemen of Verona

LOVE CAN FEED ON AIR.

Romeo and Juliet

JULIET

'TIS ALMOST MORNING; I WOULD HAVE THEE GONE:
AND YET NO FURTHER THAN A WANTON'S BIRD;
WHO LETS IT HOP A LITTLE FROM HER HAND,
LIKE A POOR PRISONER IN HIS TWISTED GYVES,
AND WITH A SILK THREAD PLUCKS IT BACK AGAIN,
SO LOVING-JEALOUS OF HIS LIBERTY.

ROMEO

I WOULD I WERE THY BIRD.

Twelfth Night

WHAT IS LOVE? 'TIS NOT HEREAFTER;
PRESENT MIRTH HATH PRESENT LAUGHTER;
WHAT'S TO COME IS STILL UNSURE:
IN DELAY THERE LIES NO PLENTY;
THEN COME KISS ME, SWEET AND TWENTY,
YOUTH'S A STUFF WILL NOT ENDURE.

Measure for Measure

WHAT'S MINE IS YOURS AND WHAT IS YOURS IS MINE.

As You Like It

THE WOUNDS INVISIBLE
THAT LOVE'S KEEN ARROWS MAKE.

MY HEART'S SUBDUED
EVEN TO THE VERY QUALITY OF MY LORD:
I SAW OTHELLO'S VISAGE IN HIS MIND,
AND TO HIS HONOUR AND HIS VALIANT PARTS
DID I MY SOUL AND FORTUNES CONSECRATE.

MIRANDA

DO YOU LOVE ME?

FERDINAND

O HEAVEN, O EARTH, BEAR WITNESS TO THIS SOUND
AND CROWN WHAT I PROFESS WITH KIND EVENT
IF I SPEAK TRUE! IF HOLLOWLY, INVERT
WHAT BEST IS BODED ME TO MISCHIEF!
I BEYOND ALL LIMIT OF WHAT ELSE I'
THE WORLD DO LOVE, PRIZE, HONOUR YOU.

Romeo and Juliet

WITH LOVE'S LIGHT WINGS DID I O'ER-PERCH THESE WALLS;
FOR STONY LIMITS CANNOT HOLD LOVE OUT,
AND WHAT LOVE CAN DO THAT DARES LOVE ATTEMPT.

MY BOUNTY IS AS BOUNDLESS AS THE SEA,
MY LOVE AS DEEP; THE MORE I GIVE TO THEE,
THE MORE I HAVE, FOR BOTH ARE INFINITE.

Twelfth Night

LOVE SOUGHT IS GOOD, BUT GIVEN UNSOUGHT IS BETTER.

SO ARE YOU TO MY THOUGHTS AS FOOD TO LIFE,
OR AS SWEET-SEASON'D SHOWERS ARE TO THE GROUND;
AND FOR THE PEACE OF YOU I HOLD SUCH STRIFE
AS 'TWIXT A MISER AND HIS WEALTH IS FOUND;
NOW PROUD AS AN ENJOYER AND ANON
DOUBTING THE FILCHING AGE WILL STEAL HIS TREASURE,
NOW COUNTING BEST TO BE WITH YOU ALONE,
THEN BETTER'D THAT THE WORLD MAY SEE MY PLEASURE;
SOMETIME ALL FULL WITH FEASTING ON YOUR SIGHT
AND BY AND BY CLEAN STARVED FOR A LOOK;
POSSESSING OR PURSUING NO DELIGHT,
SAVE WHAT IS HAD OR MUST FROM YOU BE TOOK.
THUS DO I PINE AND SURFEIT DAY BY DAY,
OR GLUTTONING ON ALL, OR ALL AWAY.

85

Page 42   Charles Robinson. from The Songs and Sonnets of William Shakespeare, 1915.
Page 44   Francesco Hayez. "The Kiss," 1859.
Page 46   N.M. Price. from Tales From Shakespeare, 1945.
Page 48   William Hatherell. from Shakespeare's Tragedy of Romeo and Juliet, 1912.
Page 50   Hugh Thomson. from Shakespeare's Comedy of As You Like It, 1909.
Page 52   W. Heath Robinson.
            from Shakespeare's Comedy of Twelfth Night or What You Will, 1914.
Page 54   Edwin Landseer. "A Midsummer Night's Dream," 1848.
Page 56   Sir John Everett Millais. "The Crown of Love," 1875.
Page 58   D.G. Rossetti. "Paolo and Francesca da Rimini" (detail), 1855.
Page 60   Florence Harrison. from Early Poems of William Morris, 1914.
Page 62   Charles Robinson. from The Songs and Sonnets of William Shakespeare, 1915.
Page 64   Florence Harrison. from Poems by Christina Rossetti, 1910.
Page 66   J.H. Bacon. from Children's Stories from Shakespeare, n.d.
Page 68   Howard Pyle. from The Line of Love, 1905.
Page 70   John Duncan. "Tristan and Isolde," 1912.
Page 72   Eleanor Fortescue Brickdale.
            from Eleanor Fortescue Brickdale's Golden Book of Songs and Ballads, c.1920's.
Page 74   Thomas Stothard. "Othello and Desdemona Reunited in Cyprus" (detail), 1810.
Page 76   Paul Woodroffe. from The Tempest, 1908.
Page 78   Ford Madox Brown. "Romeo and Juliet", 1870.
Page 80   W. H. Margetson. "Juliet," c.1939.
Page 82   Florence Harrison. from Poems by Christina Rossetti, 1910.
Page 84   Reginald L. Knowles. from Old World Love Stories, 1913.
Page 86   Hugh Thomson. from The Merry Wives of Windsor, 1910.
Page 89   Alice Havers. from A Book of Old Ballads, c.1890.

Black and White Illustration Sources:

Page 4, 7 – Arthur Rackham. from A Midsummer Night's Dream, 1908; Page 13, 29, 33, 67 – The
Gateway to Shakespeare, c.1911; Page 25 – H.C. Selous. Cassell's Illustrated Shakespeare, n..d..; Page 65,
71 – Florence Harrison. from Early Poems of William Morris, 1914; Page 55 – W. Heath Robinson. A
Midsummer Night's Dream, 1914; Page 31 – Florence Harrison. from Poems by Christina Rossetti, 1910;
Page 41, 77 – Kenny Meadows. Pearls of Shakespeare, 1860; Page 69 – Ludwig Richter. J.P. Hebel's
Allemannische Gedichte, 1851; Page 45, 49, 59, 75 – Sir John Gilbert. Sir John Gilbert's Shakespeare,
1882; Page 11, 19, 23, 37, 47, 51, 61, 83 – Sir John Gilbert. The Library Shakespeare, n.d.; Page 9, 15,
17, 21, 27, 35, 39, 53, 63, 73, 79, 81, 85, 88 – Paul Thumann. Heinrich Heine's Buch der Lieder, n.d.

THIS BOOK WAS
TYPESET IN
TRAJAN, CENTAUR
AND BICKHAM SCRIPT

&

DESIGNED AT
BLUE LANTERN STUDIO
SEATTLE